SUMMER CAMP
JOURNAL

THIS JOURNAL
BELONGS TO

_____

_____

BEST MOMENT:

FUN ACTIVITY:

CAMP LOCATION:

BEST FOOD:

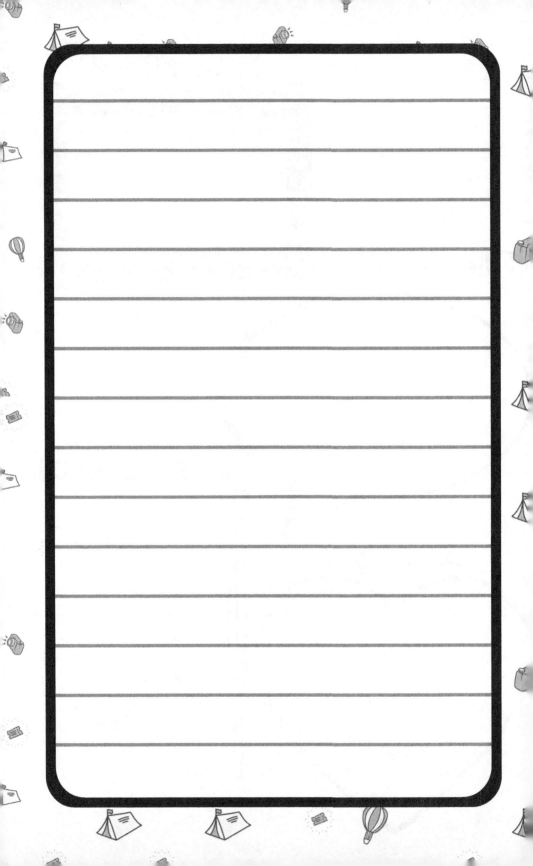

Camp Doodles

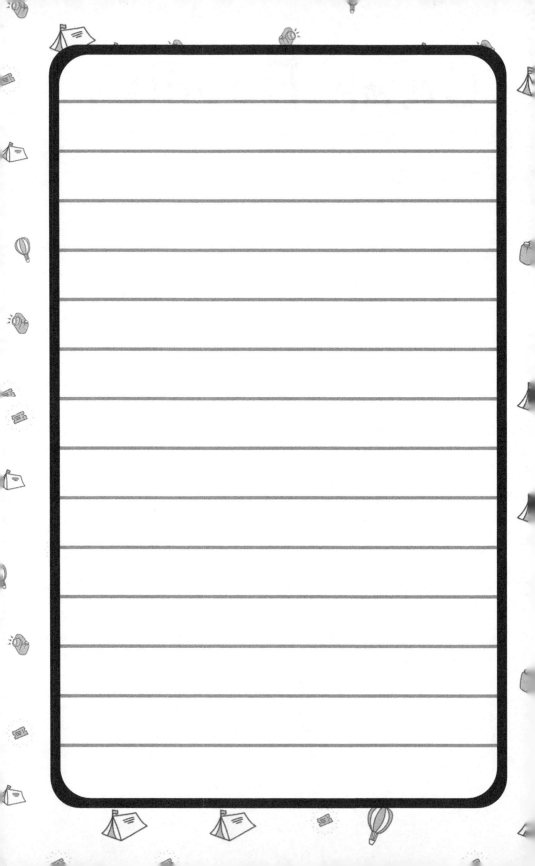

Camp Doodles

Camp Doodles

Camp Doodles

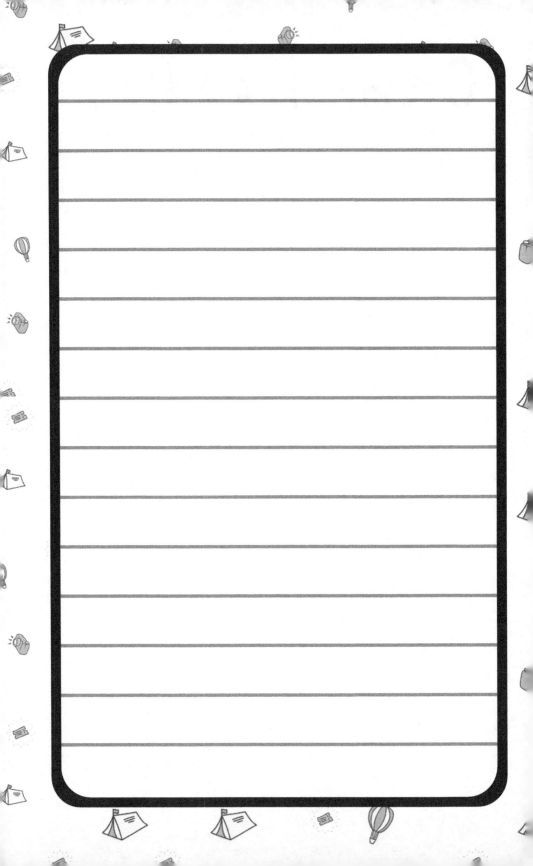

Camp Doodles

Camp Doodles

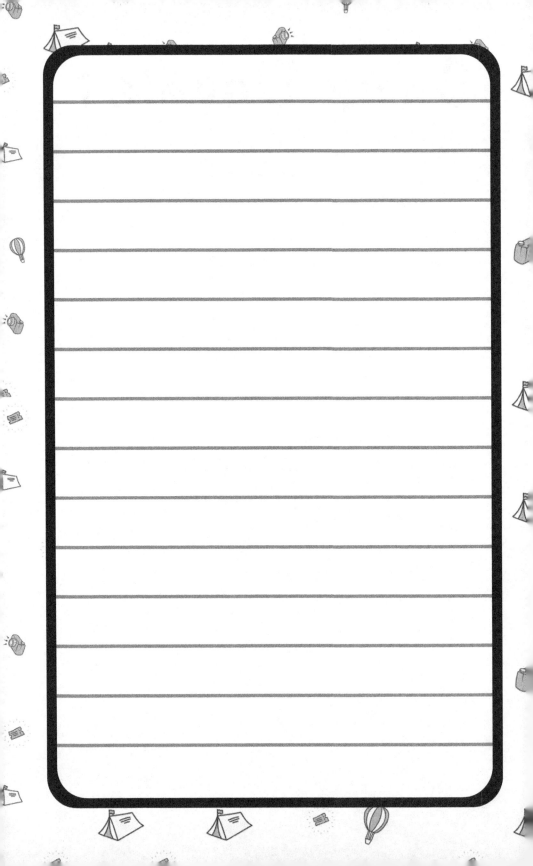

Camp Doodles

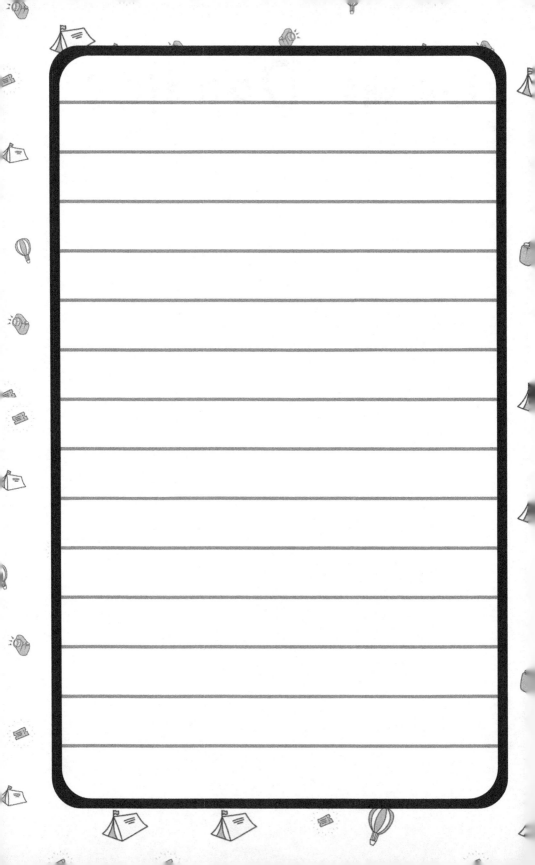

Camp Doodles

Camp Doodles

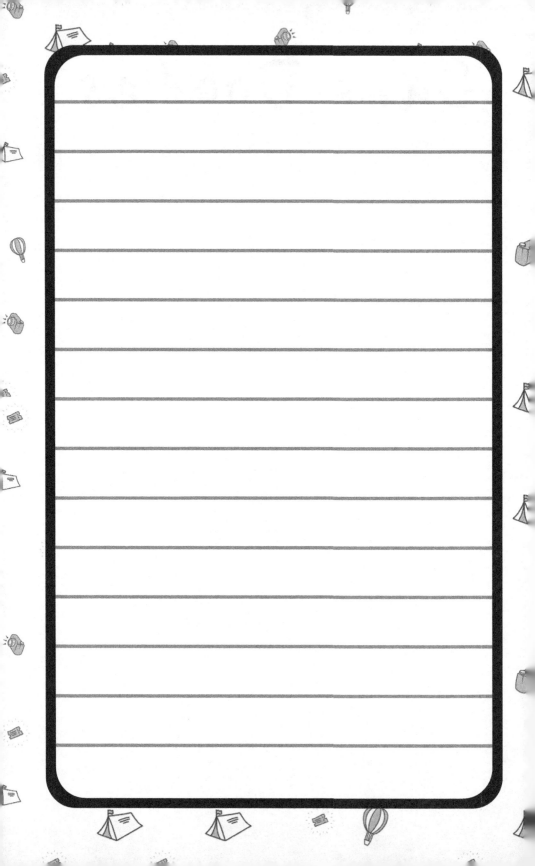

Camp Doodles

Camp Doodles

Camp Doodles

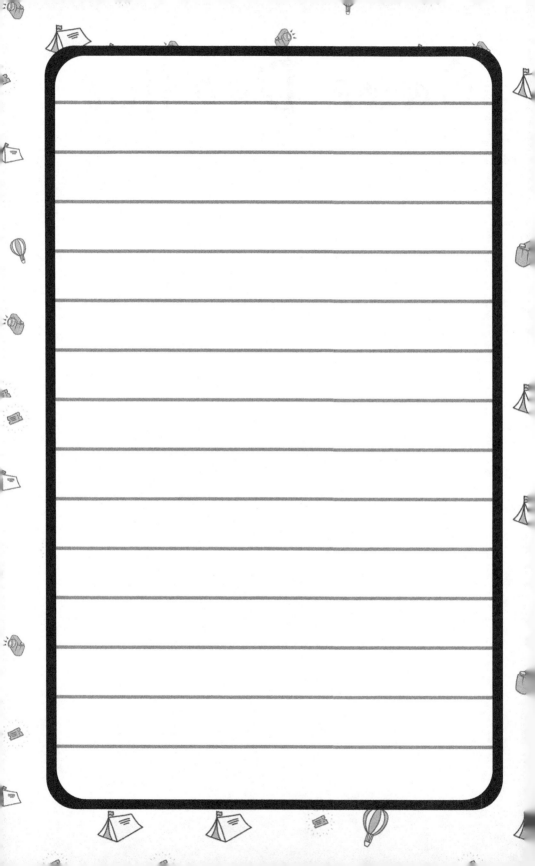

Camp Doodles

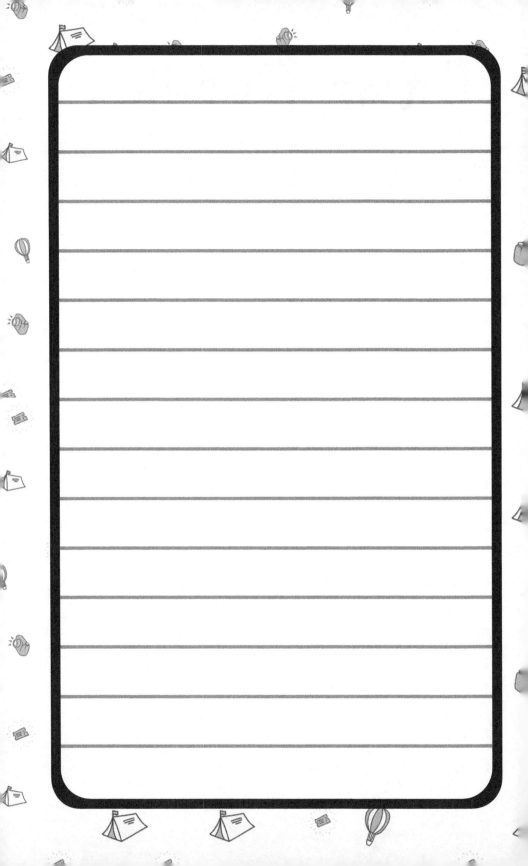

Camp Doodles

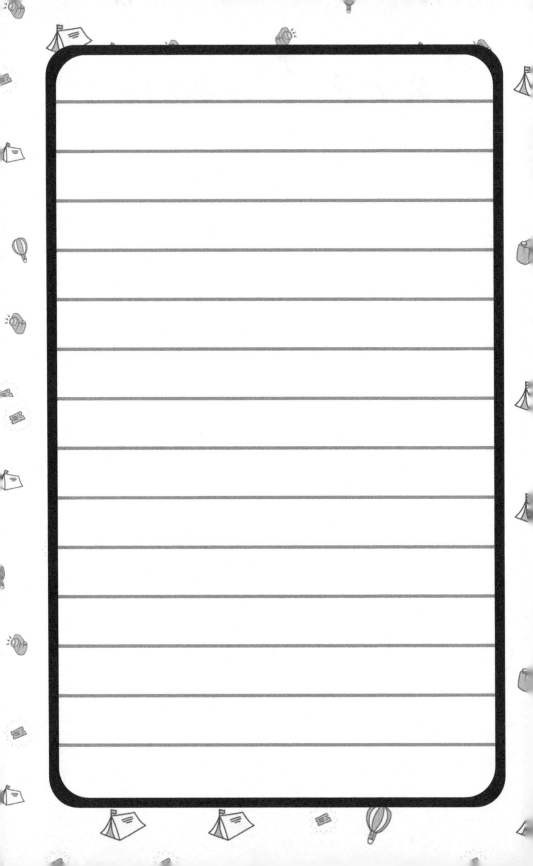

Camp Doodles

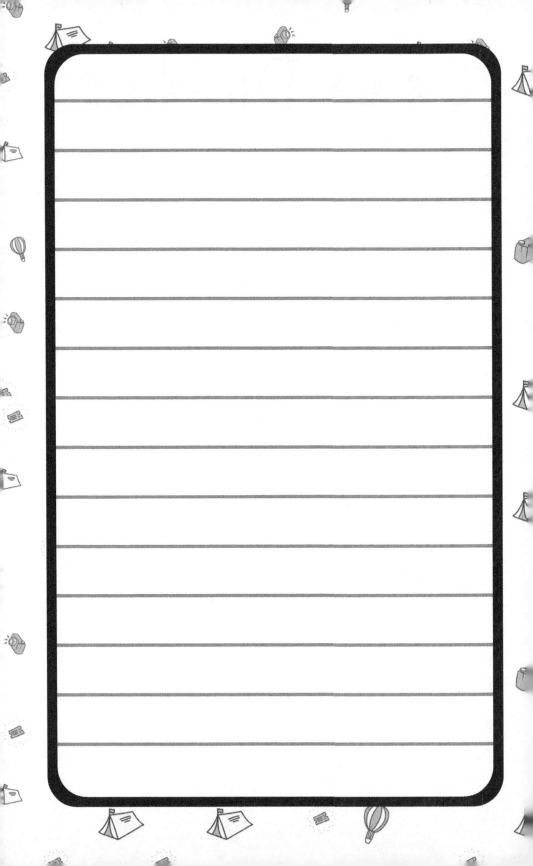

Camp Doodles

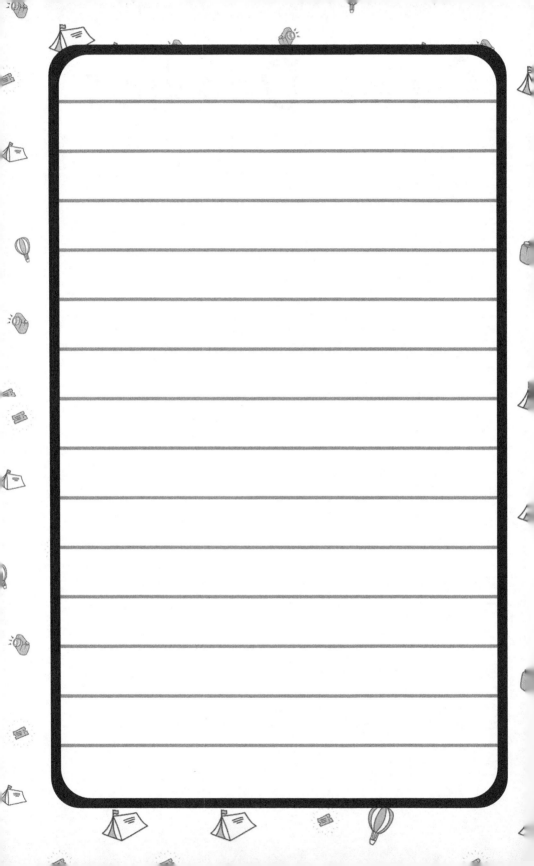

Camp Doodles

Camp Doodles

Camp Doodles

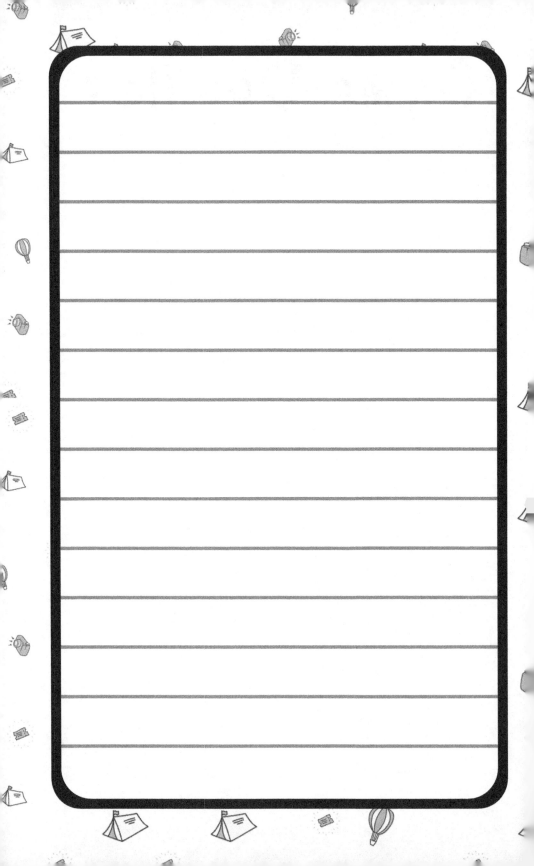

Camp Doodles

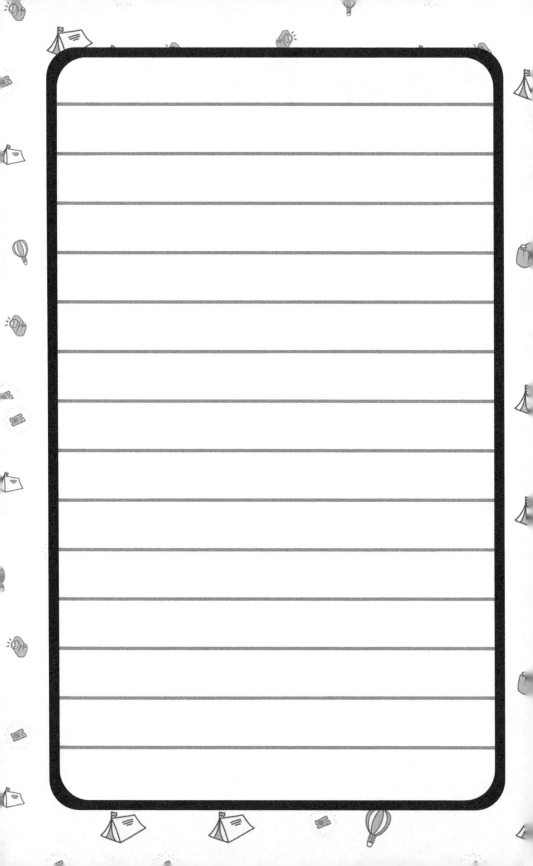

Camp Doodles

Camp Doodles

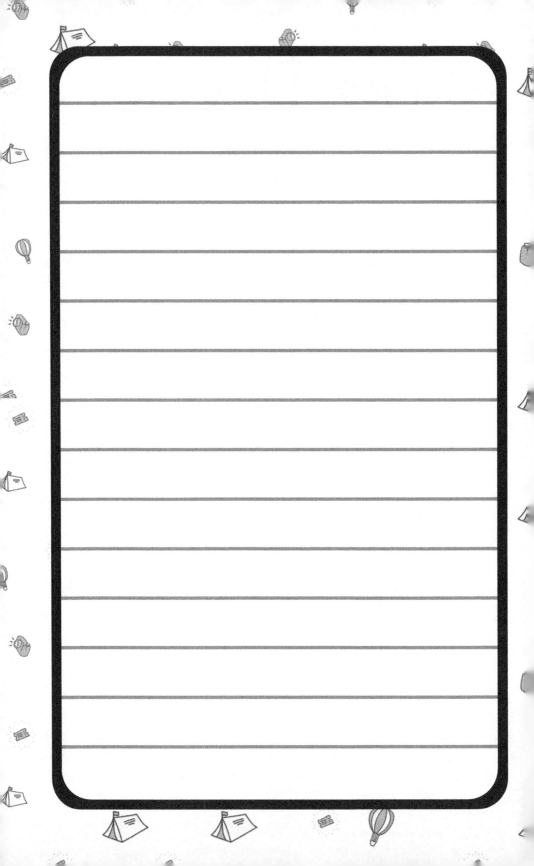

Camp Doodles

Camp Doodles

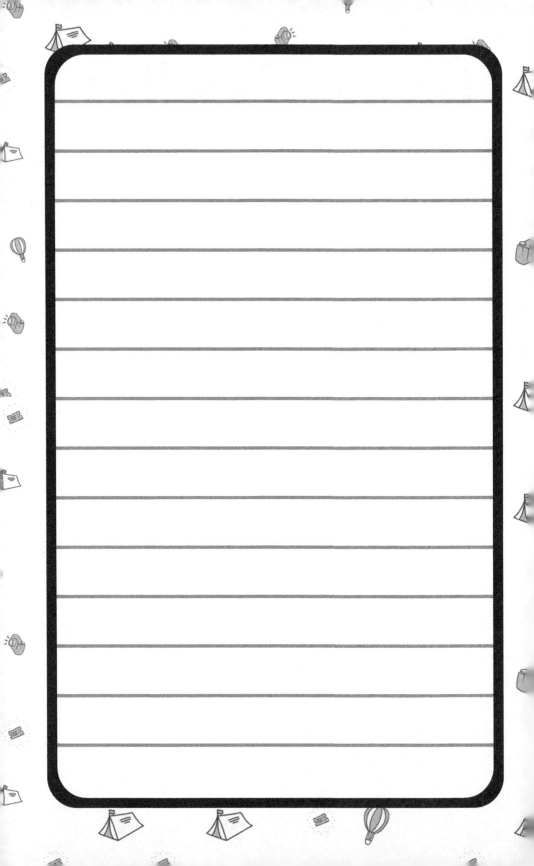

Camp Doodles

Camp Doodles

Camp Doodles

Camp Doodles

Camp Doodles

Camp Doodles

Camp Doodles

Camp Doodles

Camp Doodles

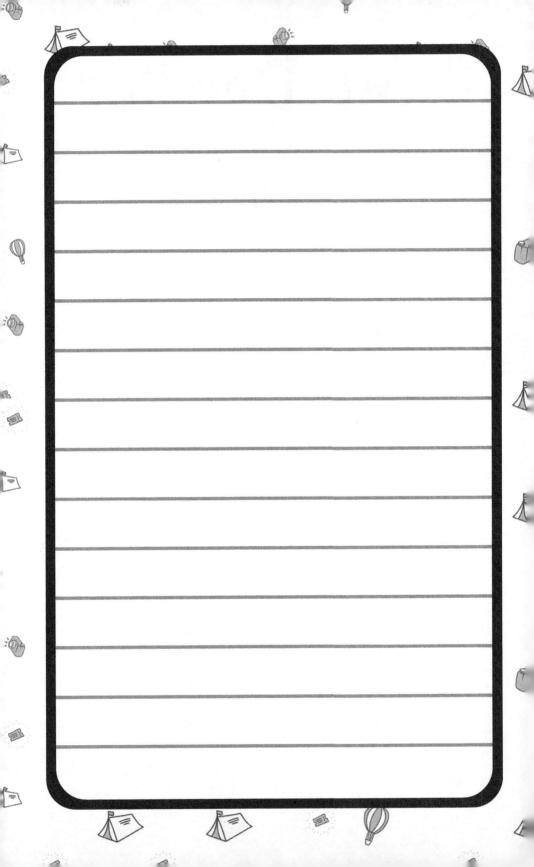

Camp Doodles

Camp Doodles

Camp Doodles

Camp Doodles

Camp Doodles

Camp Doodles

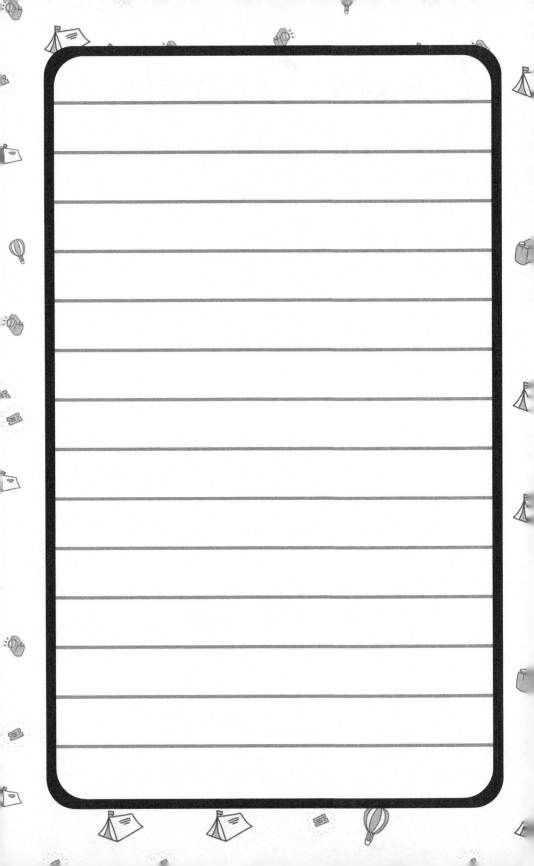

Camp Doodles

Camp Doodles

Camp Doodles

Camp Doodles

Memories in Photos

Memories in Photos

Memories in Photos

Memories in Photos

Memories in Photos

Memories in Photos

Memories in Photos

Memories in Photos

My New Friends

(sign anywhere)

My New Friends
(sign anywhere)